Everything You Need to Know About

The Dangers of Binge Drinking

Drinking is a part of our culture, but sometimes it can get out of hand.

Everything You Need to Know About The Dangers of Binge Drinking

Magdalena Alagna

The Rosen Publishing Group, Inc.
New York

Published in 2001 by The Rosen Publishing Group, Inc.
29 East 21st Street, New York, NY 10010

Library of Congress Cataloging-in-Publication Data

Alagna, Magdalena.
Everything you need to know about the dangers of binge drinking / by Magdalena Alagna. — 1st ed.
p. cm. — (Need to know library)
Includes bibliographical references and index.
ISBN 0-8239-3289-3
1. Teenage girls—Alcohol use—United States—Juvenile literature. 2. Teenage boys—Alcohol use—United States—Juvenile literature. 3. Alcoholism—United States—Prevention—Juvenile literature. [1. Alcoholism.] I. Title. II. Series.
HV5135.A383 2000
362.292—dc21

00-011256

Manufactured in the United States of America

Contents

Introduction

Some school traditions, like going to football games, are harmless. Other traditions of high school and college life can be dangerous. For example, many students don't see anything wrong with drinking twenty-one shots on their twenty-first birthday, or chugging beer from a beer bong, especially if many other teens are doing the same. But for many young people, binge drinking can be a problem.

How can you tell if someone is binge drinking? After all, people drink alcohol for many different reasons. They drink to relax, to lose their inhibitions, or to fit in with their friends. Many people drink socially and responsibly without bad consequences. However, a person who has a problem with binge drinking will drink at least five drinks in a row (four for women), drink just to get drunk, or believe that a good time cannot be had without drinking. Some binge drinkers even drink to the point of having blackouts, meaning they do not remember what happened when they were drunk. Some participate in dangerous activities, such as drinking and driving. Others may be suspended from school because of a drug- or alcohol-related incident. These are all signs that a person has a serious problem with alcohol.

The risks of binge drinking are more than just a headache the next day. Many students who drink heavily find that their grades start slipping. They might give up activities and hobbies that they used to enjoy, like sports or hanging out with friends. Others may find that their social lives are taking a turn for the worse. They may lose friends because of the things that they do or say when they have been drinking. Binge drinking can also lead to problems such as unsafe sex, violent behavior, and even arrests. Also, there are many health problems that can develop as a result of drinking too much.

Young women must be especially careful. Women are more likely to be the victims of sexual attack when they are intoxicated, meaning there is also greater risk of date rape, unplanned pregnancy, and exposure to HIV. Unfortunately, despite the risks, there are more young women who are binge drinking today than there were ten years ago.

People may not realize that binge drinking can affect students who don't drink at all. This is called the secondhand effects of binge drinking. Surveys show that nondrinking students are subjected to a greater incidence of personal assault and sexual harassment on campuses where large portions of the student body are binge drinkers. Surveys also show that those students who have a problem with binge drinking in high school are more likely to be binge drinkers in college.

What can you do to prevent binge drinking? You can know the facts about alcohol consumption. You can make the choice to keep yourself informed and to keep your mind clear and strong. People will learn from your positive example. You can even learn what to do to help a friend who may be a binge drinker, or you can get together with like-minded students and campaign to send the message to other kids that binge drinking doesn't ever pay off.

Chapter

1

What Is Binge Drinking?

*I*t was Friday night, and classes were done for the week. Michael was in a bar celebrating. He and a few friends were winding down with a couple of drinks, but a couple of drinks soon led to many more.

Michael had had a difficult week, and he felt he deserved some fun. He was especially worried about his biology exam. He had studied hard and he was pretty sure he had done well, though he was glad to forget about his troubles as he took the first sip of a cold beer.

That beer tasted so good that it was soon finished. Michael immediately got another one and downed it just as fast. He could feel all of his tensions relaxing, one by one. Michael's friend Peter

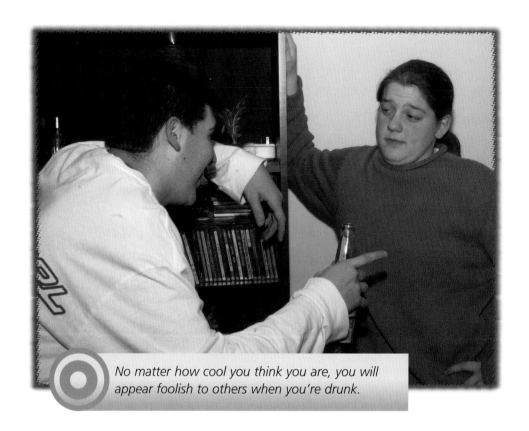

No matter how cool you think you are, you will appear foolish to others when you're drunk.

saw how quickly he was drinking and challenged him to a little contest. Peter wanted to see whether Michael could finish a beer before he did. They quickly chugged down their beers.

Michael looked across the room and saw Katie, a pretty girl from one of his classes. He wanted to go over and talk to her, but he didn't feel brave enough. He reached for another beer. Pretty soon Michael was starting to feel great. He felt full of confidence, as if he had many witty things to say. Suddenly, he was not so worried about what he would say as he walked over to talk to Katie.

"Aren't you in one of my classes?" Michael said to Katie. He felt lightheaded and happy, not worried at all.

"Biology," Katie said, giving Michael a strange look.

She thought that he might be drunk. His words were slurred, and he was weaving a little unsteadily on his feet. In fact, as Katie thought back over the last hour, she was pretty sure Michael had already had three beers, maybe more.

When Katie had seen Michael in their biology class, she had thought that he was attractive, and the comments that he made in class were intelligent. She had thought she might like to get to know him better. Now Katie was not so sure.

Many binge drinkers don't think of what they do every weekend as binge drinking. Sometimes, it's hard to pin down exactly what binge drinking is. This is especially true when you consider that you may have seen many instances in which your parents and their friends have had a few drinks to relax. They might drink a couple drinks with dinner or to celebrate a special occasion. Drinking is, in fact, an established part of our culture, and there is nothing wrong with drinking alcohol in moderation. Some health studies even show that drinking a moderate amount of alcohol—one drink per day for women, and two drinks per day for men—can thin the blood a little bit, which is a health benefit for people who have had a heart attack.

Are you a binge drinker if you want to get drunk on the weekends? Doesn't everyone go out and get drunk on the weekends? In certain situations, after all, proving your worth socially is often about how well you can handle your alcohol. Are you a binge drinker if you have a few drinks to relax? What if you regularly consume a lot of alcohol but you can still hold a job or attend all your classes? All of these questions will be answered in this chapter.

Signs of Binge Drinking

There are a few signs to watch out for when you think someone may be binge drinking. As you will see, binge drinking is different from just having one or two drinks to relax or have a good time. It is also different from alcoholism. Bingeing means drinking a lot of alcohol in a short amount of time.

The Measurements

What is considered one drink? One drink is a twelve-ounce can or bottle of beer, a twelve-ounce bottle of wine cooler, a four-ounce glass of wine, or a shot of liquor, either straight or in a mixed drink.

If you drink five alcoholic drinks in a row (four for women), you are engaging in binge drinking. It makes sense to define binge drinking using different figures for men and women. This is because research shows that women experience many of the same alcohol-related problems when binge drinking that men do—except that women have those problems after drinking four drinks, not five. If you drink this amount of alcohol three or more times in a two-week period, that is binge drinking. This is especially true if you are slamming down your drinks and actually trying to get drunk. No matter what you have seen in the movies about high school or college life, going out and getting drunk every Friday and Saturday night definitely qualifies as binge drinking. The list below features some other signs of binge drinking.

Signs of Binge Drinking

◎ Having frequent hangovers from drinking a lot at parties

◎ Drinking until you get sick or pass out

◎ Doing or saying things after drinking that you wouldn't normally do or say, or doing things that you regret the next day

◉ Feeling you must drink to have fun

◉ Noticing that a lot of your stories begin with "We were so drunk that night" or "I was so wasted"

◉ Avoiding spending time with friends who don't drink

◉ A night of drinking ends in being hospitalized with alcohol poisoning

◉ You get arrested as a result of alcohol-related behavior

◉ You frequently black out as a result of drinking

◉ You experience short-term memory loss as a result of drinking

Binge Drinking Vs. Drinking Responsibly

Just because people have a few drinks doesn't make them binge drinkers. There are people who can have a few drinks, enjoy those drinks, and still behave responsibly. They don't lose friends because of the things that they say or do when they have been drinking. They have never been convicted of DWI (driving while intoxicated) or DUI (driving under the influence), or lost their driver's licenses because of an alcohol-related incident;

nor have they been arrested. Overall, drinking does not affect the areas of their lives that really matter, like going to work or school.

Binge Drinking: Myths and Facts

Alcohol is considered an established part of our culture, and that is doubly true of high school and college life. Many movies, from classics of fraternity-house life such as *Animal House* to more recent films like *Road Trip* and *American Pie*, picture wild parties where drinking alcohol and getting drunk is the norm.

However, in reality, there are stories in the news every year about how dangerous some of the drinking rituals practiced by fraternities and sororities are. Many students lose their lives because of alcohol poisoning or drunk driving accidents. Stories about students who died of alcohol poisoning because they couldn't consume the vast amount of alcohol required by their fraternity are exposing how dangerous—even fatal—binge drinking can be. Unfortunately, these stories' impacts are not stopping students who are drinking to get drunk.

In 1999, the Harvard School of Public Health did a follow-up study to its 1993 College Alcohol Study. It found that more than 44 percent of college students engaged in binge drinking during the two weeks before the survey was done, and at almost one-third of the

Some Hollywood movies, such as Animal House, *glamorize excessive drinking.*

colleges surveyed, more than half the students were binge drinkers during those two weeks. The study also found that compared to other students, college students who were binge drinkers in high school were almost three times more likely to be binge drinkers in college. Another interesting finding was that no matter how much they drank, not too many students felt that they had a problem with alcohol. Only one-fifth of one percent called themselves problem drinkers.

On the other hand, students correctly estimated how much binge drinking there is on their campuses. At the campuses surveyed, students estimated that 35 percent of the student body engages in binge drinking. This is close to the actual figure researchers found to be the national average, which is 44 percent. That's two in every five students!

The Role of Peer Pressure

Tamika was excited that Sharon and Derek had invited her to go to a party with them at Angela's house. In school, Angela had made a big deal about how she was going to buy a keg and throw a huge bash. She also made it clear to Tamika that she didn't think Tamika had what it took to be considered a part of "her crowd." Tamika was looking forward to proving she could be as much fun as anyone else— maybe even more.

When they got to Angela's house, they saw crowds of people carrying plastic cups filled with beer. "The keg's in the kitchen!" Angela shouted over the loud music.

"Let me get you a beer," Derek said, and Tamika didn't object.

Although Tamika did not realize it, there are more subtle forms of peer pressure than making someone play a drinking game or drink a large amount of alcohol for a dare or an initiation. Although no one likes to think that he or she is doing something just to be part of the crowd, this is in fact what often happens. It is nice to feel accepted by a group and to feel as if you have a group of friends.

In fact, it is quite common for teens to find themselves doing things that they wouldn't normally do when they are surrounded by a group of "friends," especially if everyone else looks at it as no big deal. Teens can be led to drink far more than they intended to, especially if they are new to drinking alcohol and don't realize how alcohol affects them. Also, an article on binge drinking that appeared in *Seventeen* magazine cited that many girls say they are pressured to drink when they hang out with the guys. They say it isn't as common for girls to pressure each other into drinking.

Why Binge Drink?

The reasons for binge drinking are as different as are all of the people who drink to get drunk. Everyone has a different reason. Everyone has a different story. Some people do it to manage stress. Some people drink because they think that's the only way that they can have a good time, while others drink to overcome shyness in social situations. They believe drinking makes them more outgoing and talkative.

People think that drinking will help them overcome insecurity and social anxiety.

Once they have started, people continue to binge drink because they may not be aware that it is a danger. They may think that drinking to get drunk every weekend is normal and that many people live their lives that way. They don't see that it can become a problem until it's too late.

Chapter 2

Risks and Consequences

Enrique was having a great time at the party. It wasn't a big party—just a few people hanging out in someone's dorm room. He didn't even know the guy who was throwing it.

First, Enrique started with a few beers. He was feeling good and was starting to mix more with the crowd and meet more people. Then someone offered him a shot of tequila. One group of guys was drinking only tequila, making a game out of it.

Enrique knew he was getting drunk, but he didn't want to stop doing shots. He didn't even want to stop when he couldn't walk steadily back and forth to the bathroom, or when he threw up. "Now there's just more room for the tequila," he joked to his friends.

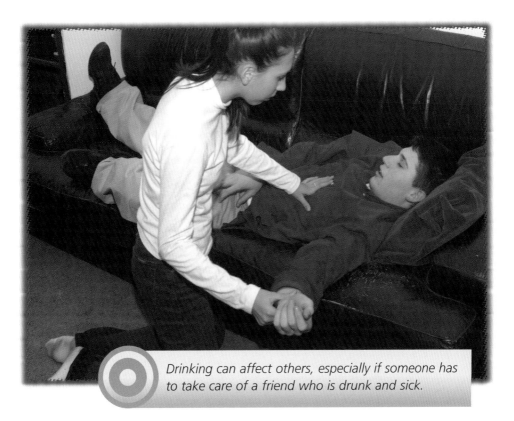

Drinking can affect others, especially if someone has to take care of a friend who is drunk and sick.

His own voice sounded funny to him. His words were coming out slurred. As he looked around the room at everyone talking, laughing, and drinking, Enrique realized that he was seeing double. It wasn't long before Enrique passed out on a chair in the corner.

When the party was starting to break up, Sherry tried to wake up Enrique. She asked him if he was okay. She shouted at him to open his eyes. She shook him by the shoulders. Enrique didn't even respond. Sherry picked up his hand and felt his wrist for his pulse. It was very fast, and the skin of his hand felt clammy. She reached for the phone and dialed 911.

No matter which way you look at it, binge drinking is risky behavior. Not only are there short-term and long-term health risks involved with binge drinking, but there is also physical and psychological damage that can result. Also, don't forget to take into account the many accidents that can happen as a result of binge drinking. Drunk driving claims thousands of lives every year, helping to make motor vehicle accidents the leading cause of death among young people.

Many people don't realize that it is possible to overdose on alcohol, which is called alcohol poisoning. Sometimes, a person can ingest so much alcohol that it can be fatal. Also, each year young people die from other alcohol-related accidents, such as choking on vomit. How about this tragic story: In 1997, an eighteen-year-old sophomore at Virginia Tech went to sleep drunk and rolled from her bed out of a dorm window, falling eight stories to her death!

Who Is at Risk?

Naturally, students who binge drink are placing themselves at risk for a number of problems, and frequent binge drinkers are the ones who have the most serious problems. One study found that frequent binge drinkers were seven to sixteen times more likely than non–binge drinkers to miss class or get behind in their schoolwork. Frequent binge drinkers were found to have engaged in unplanned sexual activity more often, and to have used protection less regularly when having sex, than non–binge drinking students. They have more frequently gotten into trouble with campus police, damaged property, or been hurt or injured while drunk.

Recurrent binge drinkers, people who binge drink often, were ten times more likely to have driven a car after drinking, and they were sixteen times more likely to have ridden in a car with a driver who was under the influence of drugs or who was drunk. This shows how dramatically a lot of alcohol can impair your good judgment!

It isn't just college students who are at risk either. Although binge drinking is just beginning to be recognized as a problem for high school students, the facts about teenage drinking are startling. Just take a look at the statistics reported in a study released by the Substance Abuse and Mental Health Services Administration (SAMHSA). This is what the study reported about adolescents ages twelve to seventeen who use alcohol:

◎ They are more likely to report behavioral problems, including aggressive or criminal behaviors.

- They are sixteen times more likely than nondrinkers to have used an illegal drug in the past month.

- They are six times as likely as nondrinkers to report skipping school.

- They are five times more likely to report running away from home.

- They are seven and a half times more likely to report that they have been arrested.

- They are three times more likely to report deliberately trying to hurt or kill themselves than students who don't drink.

In addition, binge drinkers are more likely to use alcohol as a "gateway drug." That is, those students who frequently binge drink are the ones who are more likely to try other drugs, such as marijuana or cocaine. Many people don't think of alcohol as a drug, but it is one. In fact, it can almost be considered common knowledge that it is an illegal drug for anyone who is under twenty-one. But in a national survey, 45 percent of the binge drinkers surveyed at colleges were under twenty-one.

The risks that students who rarely or never drink are exposed to by the behavior of students who drink a lot of alcohol in a very short time are called second-hand binge effects. Students can have their studying or sleep interrupted by loud parties going on in the dorms or by having to take care of a roommate who comes home drunk. Students at colleges with high levels of binge drinking were three times more likely to be pushed, hit, or sexually assaulted by drunk peers than were those at schools with a lower level of binge drinkers in their student populations.

Binge drinking can't be considered a problem just for binge drinkers anymore. Non–binge drinking students are suffering the secondhand binge effects much too often to ignore the fact that binge drinking can be a huge problem for them.

Health Risks of Alcohol Consumption

The more accustomed to drinking alcohol your body becomes, the more alcohol you need to drink to produce the same effects. This is called developing a tolerance to alcohol, and it is another danger of binge drinking. If you become used to the high you feel after having four drinks, you will soon need six or seven to re-create the same feeling. And the more alcohol that's in your system, the more pronounced are the effects of binge drinking.

Secondhand effects of binge drinking can try the patience of friends.

In small amounts, alcohol acts as a stimulant. This is why people feel a boost in their spirits after one or two drinks. They feel happier and more outgoing. But in large amounts, alcohol is a depressant—it slows down the brain and central nervous system. Eventually, bingeing on alcohol affects your judgment and leads to memory loss. The most extreme example of this is a blackout. When you black out, you don't remember what you said or did while you were drunk. Drinking alcohol also contributes to long-term memory loss because drinking on a regular basis destroys the brain cells needed for brain functions such as memory. On top of all this, alcohol is disastrous for your looks. It's terrible for your skin because it helps cause both acne and wrinkles. Also, alcohol can easily lead to weight gain because its calories are quickly absorbed.

Destroying Your Organs

Drinking a lot of alcohol puts a strain on your liver, which is the organ in your body that metabolizes, or burns up, the alcohol that goes into your bloodstream when you have been drinking. If you drink more during your binge than your liver can easily handle, the liver has to work even harder. A liver that is working normally can burn up a lot of alcohol, but if the liver has to work extra hard all the time, it becomes less efficient and less healthy. The liver gets damaged. If you drink a lot, and you do it often, the liver becomes

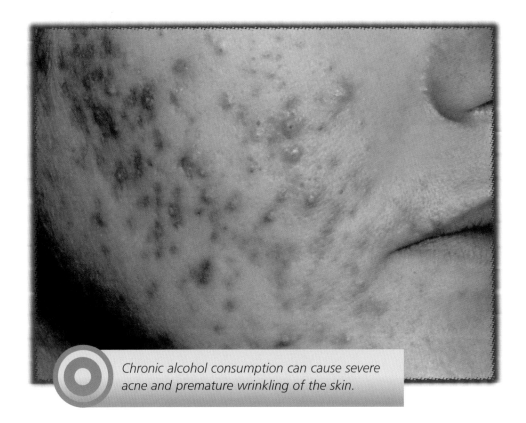

Chronic alcohol consumption can cause severe acne and premature wrinkling of the skin.

full of fat cells. The fat cells cut off the supply of blood that delivers oxygen and other nutrients to liver cells. This causes the liver cells to eventually die. They are then replaced with scar tissue. This condition is called cirrhosis.

There are a few other long-term health risks associated with the use of alcohol. It is often a contributing factor to deaths from heart disease and cancer. Let's face it—alcohol isn't terribly good for any of the organs or systems of the body. In fact, it harms almost every one of them. Not only is it the biggest cause of disease in the liver and pancreas, but it is also a factor in high blood pressure and stroke.

Consequences of Binge Drinking

Many students don't see a problem with having a few beers every once in a while. But how many is "a few," and how often is "once in a while?" When we are talking about binge drinking, the consequences of this risky behavior become very clear. Studies show that alcohol is a factor in 66 percent of student suicides and 60 percent of all sexually transmitted diseases, including HIV. In addition, one out of four student deaths is related to alcohol use.

One national study shows that students who binge drink experience a higher rate of educational, social, and health problems than their peers who do not binge drink. Half of these frequent binge drinkers report having five or more different alcohol-related problems during the school year. That's nearly twenty times the number of those kinds of problems reported by students who drink but do not binge. The message is clear: If you are over the age of twenty-one and you decide to drink alcohol, drink in moderation.

One of the most important consequences of binge drinking is the effect that it has on your grades. In one national survey, half of binge drinkers report that they missed at least one class as a result of their alcohol use, and more than a third say they fell behind in their schoolwork. Binge drinkers are also more likely to report lower grades than non–binge drinkers do.

There are also social problems that come with binge drinking. In the beginning, the binge drinker will feel relaxed, confident, witty, and outgoing after having a few drinks. He or she may also find a group of friends who are interested in binge drinking. For a time, it might seem as if binge drinking is a big social scene, a sure method to gaining and keeping popularity.

Actually, the opposite is true. People enjoy the lack of inhibition that comes with drinking alcohol. They think it contributes to making friends. But it can actually ruin friendships. Many binge drinkers report that they have either said or done something while drinking that they regretted the next day. This could be anything from having a fight with a good friend to scaring off a potential romantic partner because of how you act when you are drunk.

Finally, students who binge drink are more likely to be in trouble with the campus police or be arrested for a whole range of reasons—public drunkenness, fights, vandalism, or disturbing the peace. These experiences could lead to expulsion from school if they happen too often.

As we mentioned, binge drinking can also lead to drunk driving. One national study showed that frequent binge drinkers were ten times more likely than non–binge drinkers to have driven after drinking alcohol, and they were sixteen times more likely than non–binge drinkers to have ridden with a driver who

Binge drinking can hurt your brain and your grades.

was high or drunk. In addition to the fact that people can get seriously injured or killed in drunk driving accidents, there is the whole legal catastrophe of being stopped by a cop after you have been binge drinking. In fact, there are stiffer fines being given all the time for drunk driving. In many states, you can lose your license for six months to a year, and you also will have to participate in community service. You could even have your insurance canceled or spend some time in jail! This is especially true if you cause a death or a serious injury in an accident, or if you are involved in more than one accident.

Binge drinking also increases the likelihood that women will suffer the disastrous effects of binge drinking, even if they themselves are not binge drinkers. Up until now, we've only briefly discussed the incidence of date rape, sexual assault, and the many problems that can result, such as unplanned pregnancy or contracting a sexually transmitted disease. The numbers for sexual assault and the transmission of HIV from incidents of sexual assault are growing. The next chapter deals specifically with how binge drinking affects women.

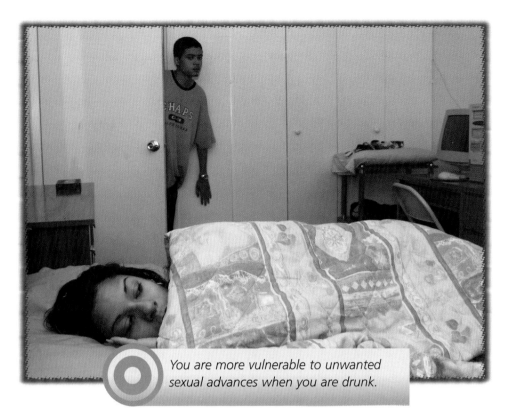

You are more vulnerable to unwanted sexual advances when you are drunk.

had been staring at her that night, she felt afraid. She started to panic. She didn't know this guy at all.

Jodie thought about how she'd been so sure that she could protect herself. She hadn't planned on getting so drunk. But it had been hard to say no when people were so friendly and the conversation and the alcohol were flowing. She'd had five drinks without even really being aware of it, and now she was alone in a room with a stranger.

She could barely think straight. The party was so loud downstairs that no one would hear her, *even if she screamed. There was no other way out except the door, and he was standing in front of it.*

Sexual Assault and Date Rape

When talking about sexual assault, it is important to remember that the statistics and figures that have been gathered, although frightening enough, can't adequately reflect how often these incidents occur. Unwanted sexual advances, sexual assault, and date rape happen much more frequently than anyone wants to imagine. Often these incidents are not reported because binge drinking and use of the date rape drug Rohypnol can make it difficult to remember exactly what went on.

Many incidents of date rape are not reported because women wake up in frat houses the next day without their clothes and just don't remember how they got there. And many incidents of rape are not taken to court because many women do not have the resources available, such as a rape crisis center in their area or at their local hospital. Another reason rape cases may not be taken to court is that the local judicial system sometimes claims that there isn't enough money to provide staff to investigate and bring to court even a decent number of those incidents that are reported.

If you have been raped, go straight to the police and report it. Have them take blood and urine samples. They may need those things for evidence in building a case against your attacker. Don't go to the police alone. Have a friend, a parent, or even a lawyer go with you.

You should also go to the doctor. This is because, in addition to the disastrous psychological effects of being raped, there are also many health problems that could result. Unplanned pregnancy or a sexually transmitted disease are just two of these. Sexually transmitted diseases range in severity from those that can be treated with penicillin, such as gonorrhea, to fatal diseases for which there is no cure, such as AIDS, which can result from contracting HIV. If you have been the victim of date rape, it is vital that you get a gynecological exam. Many sexually transmitted diseases can be treated if they are diagnosed in time. But many of these diseases do not have any symptoms until you are in the advanced stages of the disease, meaning you could have a sexually transmitted disease and not even know it. Some of these diseases, such as gonorrhea, could make you sterile—unable to have children—if they are not treated in time.

If you need more information about what to do if you are raped, or if you have been raped and want to seek out counseling, please check the resources section at the back of this book for more information.

Unwanted Sexual Advances

Binge drinking also increases your chances of not being able to fend off an unwanted sexual advance because drinking large amounts of alcohol affects your motor coordination—how you walk, talk, and move. How are you going to fight off a man who is bigger and heavier than you are if you can't even walk in a straight line to the bathroom? You might not be able to fight off someone bigger than you, even if you haven't been drinking, but having all of your wits and your strength about you makes it that much more likely that you will be able to protect yourself. Keeping yourself alert and strong gives you at least a fighting chance.

Think about it: When you are drunk, you are not seeing or thinking clearly, and so it is harder to judge the danger of a situation. Many young women feel pleased when having a few drinks relaxes their inhibitions and makes conversation easier, especially with the opposite sex. They may think that having a drink in their hand looks glamorous. Nothing could be further from the truth. Don't forget that it is called date rape because, many times, your escort for the evening, the guy who is being so charming to you, is the one who is the rapist.

A Higher Risk

Even those young women who drink responsibly are at risk for the second-hand effects of binge drinking. The number of women subjected to unwanted sexual advances by men who have been binge drinking is shocking. In one study, the percentage of women who have had to fight off an unwanted sexual advance ranged from 15 percent at low–binge drinking colleges to 26 percent at colleges where there were large populations of binge-drinking students.

Sometimes, unwanted attention may come in the form of lewd and insulting comments. Other times, it is nothing short of rape.

Although no one wants to blame the victim in a situation of date rape, it is imperative that women look out for their own welfare. Women must remain absolutely aware and alert in situations that could quickly become dangerous for them. There are too many statistics about date rape at fraternity or sorority parties or at high school keg parties to ignore the fact that these are situations during which women have to take extreme precautions. Do not put yourself in a vulnerable

College fraternity parties may look like fun,. but you may become an easy target for a rapist if you are drunk.

position by binge drinking! Many women believe that date rape can't happen to them—until it does.

Remember, if you want to go to a party and have a few drinks, it is a good idea to bring a friend with you, for several reasons. It is smart to have a designated driver, a friend who will agree to remain sober so that she can drive home. Even if you are walking to the party, it's a good idea to have a friend who will not be drinking so that she can look out for you.

Roofies and Other Date Rape Drugs

If you are going to have a few drinks at a party, always get drinks for yourself. Do not accept drinks

That drink might contain more than alcohol—don't accept drinks from strangers or those you don't trust.

from strangers. The drug Rohypnol, or "roofies," has been getting a lot of press lately as the date rape drug of choice. This is a tasteless and odorless drug, so it is difficult to detect if it is in your drink. It acts as a sedative, a drug that slows down your body, and its effects are similar to how you feel when you are drunk. Remember that alcohol in large doses is a depressant, which also slows down your body. If you feel dizzy, if your speech is slurred, if you are having trouble walking, and you know that you have not had enough alcohol to become drunk, leave the party immediately and go to a place where you are safe. If you can, get someone to go with you. This person should be a trusted

Research indicates that women who drink alcohol, even moderately, may have an increased risk of breast cancer.

friend. Do not accept help from a stranger. He may be the person who put the drug in your drink.

If you think you may have been given a roofie, it is also a good idea to go to a medical center. When you mix a sedative like Rohypnol with alcohol, your body could slow down to the point where you stop breathing. You could die from a combination of roofies and alcohol.

Your Body, Your Health, and Alcohol

The health risks of alcohol for women are made even greater by the excessive alcohol consumption associated with binge drinking. Even women who drink a moderate amount of alcohol (that's one drink per day for women who are over twenty-one) are at a greater risk for breast cancer, in particular, and for cancers of all kinds. They are also at a greater risk for cirrhosis, a disease that affects the liver. Add to this a greater incidence of stroke and the many birth defects that could result from drinking during pregnancy, and this is one strong message for women: Consume alcohol moderately, if at all.

It's clear that binge drinking is a serious issue. What can you do to make sure that everyone knows about the dangers of binge drinking? What can you do to help a friend who is a binge drinker?

Chapter 4

What You Can Do About Binge Drinking

*U*p until the time Gina lost her best friend, Eric, she didn't see a problem with drinking alcohol. They had a lot of fun together, especially when they were drinking. It didn't matter that they were both in high school and that legally neither one of them was allowed to drink. There were plenty of ways to get alcohol when they wanted it. Eric had an older brother who got alcohol for him whenever he asked him to.

One night, Eric, who had been drinking, challenged a friend to a drag race. He wanted to show off the new sports car his parents had just bought him. Eric never finished the race. Instead the race finished him—he was involved in a fatal

Displays like this try to persuade teens and adults not to drink and drive.

car accident. He was seventeen years old and two months shy of his high school graduation.

At first, Gina didn't know how she could ease her grief. She got really angry when she overheard kids talking about how much fun it was to get drunk—especially when those people talked about drinking and driving. But lots of kids didn't seem to take seriously any of the posters or the slogans that were put up around the school by groups such as MADD—Mothers Against Drunk Driving.

Gina wanted to find a way to reach people and bring home the dangers of binge drinking. First, Gina talked to her friends and Eric's friends. She

MADD
TWENTY YEARS OF MAKING A DIFFERENCE
2000
20 years = 183,000 Lives Saved

Millie Webb, president of MADD, holds up a picture of her nineteen-month-old nephew, who was killed by a drunk driver.

explained her wish to make students aware of the dangers of binge drinking. She asked these people for their ideas about how they could get the message out. They made a list of ideas, and they talked about what might work. In the end, they decided to form an after-school club. This club would be devoted to making students aware of the dangers of binge drinking. The club also would work to provide safe and fun alternatives for students—alternatives to drinking. The club would organize events on the weekends that students could attend instead of parties where drinking would be going on.

Gina's club did many things in addition to planning alcohol-free events. They wrote letters to school and government officials outlining the dangers of binge drinking and encouraging stricter enforcement of laws against underage drinking, alcohol sold to minors, and drunk driving. They sponsored a poster contest for the best "no binge drinking" poster. They organized a peer-counselor program for kids who wanted more information about the dangers of drinking, or for kids who just wanted to talk. Gina was proudest of the ride-home program that her group organized for the prom. The group made sure that those students who wanted to have a safe ride home could get one. The group had a volunteer staff of drivers ready to provide safe rides home, waiting outside the prom like a taxi service.

Gina found that, in addition to all of the great work that her group was doing to help other students, she could handle her grief a lot better when she had something positive to focus on. She could keep the memory of her friend alive by making sure that no one else had to go through the same experiences that she and Eric had.

Few binge drinkers consider themselves to have a problem with alcohol. Not all binge drinkers have the same patterns of drinking, nor do they have the same symptoms or consequences. Reading this book, you have learned a few of the signs of a binge drinker. You know what to look for.

Keep in mind that many people who have a problem with binge drinking will start out saying that they are having a great time, that going out all the time and drinking is doing wonders for their state of mind and for their social lives. They may not see the error of their ways until they have developed a chronic health problem or unless something serious, like flunking a class, getting expelled from school, or getting arrested, makes them wake up and pay attention to what binge drinking has been doing to their lives.

Important Clues

So that people will not find out about their problem, many people who binge drink will spend less and less time with those friends who do not also binge drink. If you have a friend who is avoiding you in order to go out with people who drink themselves silly every weekend, and if that friend of yours doesn't see much of a problem with that, those are two important clues: Your friend may have a problem with binge drinking.

Even if your friend does realize that he or she has a problem with binge drinking, it may be tough for him or her to admit it. People don't like to admit to problems with alcohol. This is in part because alcohol is such a significant part of our culture and our social lives that people don't like it to look as if they can't handle the social drinking that is going on all around them. Your friend may also feel that if he stops binge drinking, he will lose all of his friends. It is a good idea to point out that if he continues to binge drink, he is in danger of losing the people who really care about him, and that if he stops binge drinking, he stands to lose only some drinking buddies.

What Can You Do to Help?

It is possible to offer help to a friend who has a problem with binge drinking. The first step a person needs to take in order to get help is to admit that he or she has a problem, and this is often the hardest step of all. What you can do is encourage your friend to talk to you about his or her drinking. It may help to get another friend to do this with you. An intervention is when a group of friends and relatives get together and confront someone they care for about his or her drinking problem. Many times during an intervention, each participant explains to the addicted person how drinking affects the person's life and the lives of everyone who cares for him or her.

Even a sweet, innocent-looking teenager like this one can be a menace to society when she drinks and drives.

Here are some tips to remember when doing an intervention:

◉ Make sure that your friend is sober while you are talking to him or her.

◉ Tell your friend that you are worried about him or her.

◉ Don't tell your friend you think he or she is an alcoholic.

◉ Don't blame him or her for binge drinking.

◉ Remind your friend of things that you may have seen him or her doing when drunk.

◉ Keep your voice full of friendship and concern, not pity or anger.

◉ Tell your friend where to go to get help. Check the resources section at the back of this book for groups that deal with helping people who have a problem with substance abuse.

◉ If you offer to go with him or her to a support group, then be prepared to do it.

◉ Make sure your friend knows that you are doing this because you are worried about him or her and because you care about his or her life.

Remember that your friend will probably deny the problem at first. It is also quite likely that he or she will be angry with you for bringing up the topic. Your friend may give you excuses for why he or she needs to drink. He or she may even blame the problem on other people, or deny the problem entirely.

If your friend does not want to seek help, you may have to seek help for him or her from a parent, guardian, teacher, or counselor. Such people might have good ideas on how to approach your friend to offer their help and concern. Even if your friend doesn't want you to say anything to these people, and even if he or she is mad at you for speaking to them, you may have to do it anyway. Remember that binge drinking causes people to take risks that can be fatal. The best way to be a friend is to tell someone who can help your friend.

Counseling

The next step that your friend faces, after admitting that he or she has a problem, is for him or her to talk to a counselor. There are many counselors who are skilled in helping people who have a problem with substance abuse. A counselor will help your friend to get back on track, and to learn why he or she is dependent on binge drinking. Often, school guidance counselors can recommend counselors who have a great amount of experience dealing with young people who have substance abuse problems. You also can look in the resources section at the back of this book for organizations that can either provide counseling or give you tips about how to locate a good counselor.

Taking Care of Yourself, Too

It can be a very trying experience to deal with someone who has a drinking problem. This is why it's incredibly important to talk to someone about the way you're feeling. There are plenty of groups out there for people who are close to someone who is addicted to alcohol. It's tough to remain closc to and to love someone who is recovering, or just beginning to recover, from a substance abuse problem.

As you know, people who have a problem with binge drinking often behave in ways that can make you very confused. For example, it's upsetting when your friend withdraws from you to spend time with his or her binge-drinking friends. But remember, you aren't alone! There are others out there who know just what you are going through, and it will help you to talk about your thoughts and feelings with them. Again, please see the resources section in the back of this book for more information on groups that can help.

There are many fun things to do with your friends that do not include binge drinking.

Setting a Positive Example

There are many things that you can do to set a positive example for a friend who has a problem with binge drinking. You can be persistent about encouraging your friend to do fun things with you—things that don't involve binge drinking.

You can also be an activist against binge drinking. Working to do something to change an existing problem and working to fight for a cause in which you believe are two great positive examples that you can set for your friend. You might even want to start an after-school club devoted to making people aware of the dangers of binge drinking. You could hold Friday night events at school to give students an alternative to going out drinking on the weekends. Students definitely will be more likely to listen to a peer when it comes to talking about drinking, so you could start a peer-counseling group. You can help yourself and help others by becoming a leader in the cause of reclaiming your youth, your energy, your life, and your choices.

Glossary

alcoholism Chronic disease characterized by physical and psychological dependence on alcohol.

alcohol poisoning A condition in which a person has consumed more alcohol than his or her body can digest.

binge drinking The consumption of five or more alcoholic drinks in a row (four for women), over a short period of time.

blackout A dulling or loss of vision, consciousness, or memory due to the ingestion of alcohol.

date rape Sexual assault upon a woman by a man who is known to her.

depressant A substance that slows down the way the body works.

drug A substance that when ingested, changes a
  person's physical or emotional state through its
  effects on the body.

drunk A slang term for being intoxicated
  with alcohol.

gateway drug A drug whose use is believed to
  lead to the use of other drugs.

inhibitions Thoughts or feelings that
  prevent a person from acting in a free and
  spontaneous way.

intervention A meeting between a person and his
  or her friends and relatives to encourage a person
  to seek help with substance abuse.

intoxicated Having enough alcohol in the bloodstream to interfere with judgment, behavior, or
  physical activity; the legal definition of intoxica-
  tion is set by statute.

Rohypnol A sedative—a drug that slows down
  your body—that is tasteless and odorless; also
  known as the date rape drug.

secondhand binge effects The effects of binge
  drinking on those people who do not binge drink.

stimulant A substance that speeds up the way the
  body works.

tolerance A reduced susceptibility to a drug's effects.

Where to Go for Help

In the United States

Al-Anon/Alateen Family Group Headquarters
1600 Corporate Landing Parkway
Virginia Beach, VA 23454-5617
(800) 4AL-ANON (425-2666) (United States.)
(800) 443-4525 (Canada)
Web site: http://www.al-anon.org

Alcoholics Anonymous
Grand Central Station
P.O. Box 459
New York, NY 10163
(212) 870-3400
Web site: http://www.alcoholics-anonymous.org

Friday Night Live
California Friday Night Live Partnership
2637 West Burrel, P.O. Box 5091
Visalia, CA 93278-5091
(559) 733-6496
e-mail: mja@tcoe.k12.ca.us
Web site: http://www.fridaynightlive.org

National Association of Teen Institutes (NATI)
c/o CADA
433 Metairie Road, Suite 306
Metairie, LA 70005
(504) 834-4357
e-mail: nati@teeninstitute.org
Web site: http://www.teeninstitute.org

National Clearinghouse for Alcohol and
        Drug Information
P.O. Box 2345
Rockville, MD 20847-2345
(800) 729-6686
e-mail: info@health.org
Web site: http://www.health.org

Youth Crisis Hotline
(800) 448-4663

In Canada

Alcohol and Drug Dependency Information and
     Counseling Services (ADDICS)
2471 1/2 Portage Avenue, #2
Winnipeg, MB R3J ON6
(204) 942-4730

Canadian Centre on Substance Abuse
75 Albert Street, Suite 300
Ottawa, ON K1P 5E7
(613) 235-4048
Web site: http://www.ccsa.ca

Canadians for Safe & Sober Driving
P.O. Box 397
Station A
Brampton, ON L6V 2L3
(905) 793-4233
e-mail: add@attcanada.ca
Web site: http://www.add.ca

For Further Reading

Aaseng, Nathan. *Teens and Drunk Driving.* San Diego, CA: Lucent Books, 2000.

Bichler, Christine. *Teen Drinking.* New York: The Rosen Publishing Group, Inc., 2000.

Grosshandler, Janet. *Drugs and Driving.* New York: The Rosen Publishing Group, Inc., 1998.

Landau, Elaine. *Hooked: Talking About Addictions.* Brookfield, CT: Millbrook Press, 1995.

Ryan, Elizabeth. *Straight Talk About Drugs and Alcohol.* Rev. ed. New York: Facts on File, Inc., 1996.

Wolff, Lisa. *Issues in Alcohol.* San Diego, CA: Lucent Books, 1999.

Index

About the Author
Magdalena Alagna is a writer and editor living in New York City.

Photo Credits
Cover and pp. 10, 19, 21, 26, 35 by Antonio Mari; p. 2 © Lichtenstein/The Image Works, Inc.; p. 16 © The Everett Collection; p. 28 © National Medical Slide; p. 31 © Scott Suchman/Pictor; p. 40 © Paul A. Souders/Corbis; p. 41 © Jim McGuire/Index Stock Imagery; p. 42 © Katie Deits/Index Stock Imagery; p. 45 © Philip Gould/Corbis; p. 46 © AP/Wide World Photos; p. 50 © SW Production/Index Stock Imagery; p. 54 © Jim Sugar Photography/Corbis.

Design and Layout
Thomas Forget